OCCASIONS of PRAYER

Lisa Withrow earned a Divinity degree
from Duke University, North Carolina,
and a PhD in Practical Theology from
the University of Glasgow. She was
ordained, and served a Church of
Scotland parish in Glasgow for four
years before returning to the United
States to minister.

Lisa writes liturgy and teaches
worship at conferences and seminars.
She also trains congregations nationally
to develop small group missional
ministries as a foundation for church
revitalization. She is currently working
with the Commission on the Status
and Role of Women to introduce
international legislation on sexual
ethics policies in the church.

She published *Seasons of Prayer* with
SPCK. *Occasions of Prayer* is her second
resource book.

OCCASIONS of PRAYER

Resources for Prayerful Living

LISA WITHROW

United Church Press
Cleveland, Ohio

United Church Press, Cleveland, Ohio 44115

Copublished with the
Society for Promoting Christian Knowledge, London, England

© 1999 by Lisa R. Withrow

Printed in Great Britain

04 03 02 01 00 99 5 4 3 2 1

ISBN 0-8298-1365-9

CONTENTS

— CONTENTS —

— CONTENTS —

— CONTENTS —

— CONTENTS —

ACKNOWLEDGEMENTS

As always, I am grateful for the stories people share with me – some joyful, some deeply painful, and many spanning the spectrum in between. These stories, and the feelings and issues connected with them, inspired this prayer resource book. The reader will encounter all kinds of moods and situations which might touch a chord – for most human feeling and experience is common to us all.

Special thanks to the Reverend Jennifer Macrae who expressed a desire to have this kind of resource book available to her in her ministry. She herself has shown me the gift of inspiration and vision in prayers we have shared over the years.

Thanks also to Rita Henderson whose eyes and spirit show me beauty and hope in life no matter what comes my way.

Finally, gratitude goes to Patricia Willis who sensitively asks the right questions at the right times.

PREFACE

Prayer can be known as a posture we take before God. 'Posture' often refers to the way we sit or stand, the way we carry ourselves physically; yet posture is also a mental self-carrying, a mental stance we take in the world. Prayer posture introduces the spiritual element of stance in the presence of God.

Praying can be one of the most vulnerable acts a person undertakes. Prayer opens the heart and mind to possibility, and kindles a desire to speak with God at the deepest level a human being can know. In addition, prayer offers a listening posture, where God has the opportunity to speak and guide. Some of the most meaningful, moving prayers are prayers of silence.

Today, most personal praying seems to happen when individuals are participating in liturgy or in simple conversation with God outside an institutional setting. When a church uses liturgy containing an abundance of words for prayer, speaking for everyone in language that may not have been examined for decades, the possibility for meaningful connection with God often diminishes. Corporate, institutional prayer may remind human beings who they are and why they come together, yet increasingly this is *not* the means by which people choose to reach into the depths of their beings to communicate with God. The postures of joy, anger, sorrow, sadness and thanksgiving frequently happen in the presence of family, friend, support group, church visitor or when a person is alone.

Occasions of Prayer is a resource book focusing specifically on life's passages, as well as life's celebrations and adversities. It may enhance pastoral visitation and can be used in small groups or individually. The prayers attempt to address situations in life where prayer postures may differ from those dictated by church liturgy or daily prayer routine.

These prayers are intentionally simple, sometimes rhythmic, reminiscent of the Celtic prayer style recently made popular again. The impact of prayer is stronger when there are fewer words filling in potentially silent places. Silence allows for creative hearing or unarticulated feeling to open itself to be expressed in God's presence. Reading with cadence and frequent pauses allows greater connection of thought and feeling with God.

People respond with emotion when using these resources. Their responses also show relief that words and presence which they had difficulty finding are actually available to them. I would invite leaders or individuals to adapt resources as required in various settings by editing lines that do not fit, keeping silence when appropriate, reading together and substituting names to personalize the liturgy or prayer.

These prayers come as an offering to you, inviting creative prayer postures before God, inviting holy connection and deep meaning on the journey of faith.

Part One

RITES OF PASSAGE

INTRODUCTION

Rites of passage are times in life when significant transitions occur. All of humanity shares birth and death, while other passages may vary from person to person. Each life-change signifies a possibility for developing stronger relationship with God and companions. Feelings evoked during times of change can be articulated in prayer or simply expressed in silence. Either way, for the one who prays, acknowledging each transition before God allows for intentional holy connection. In times of transition as well as stability, then, prayer becomes an integral part of living.

The prayers in this section are short and general. Each may include other people joining in with their own words. Names may be substituted for 'this one' or 'Your servant' or 'this child' to personalize expressions during prayer. A few suggested Scripture readings may be incorporated into group or individual prayer time. May God show us the way to prayer!

BIRTH

Scripture: 1 Samuel 1.19–20, 26–8; Psalm 8; Luke 1.47–55

Thanksgiving (1) (*unison or one voice*)

For this new life –
eyes opening
ears hearing
lungs breathing
fingers touching –
for this new life
we give You thanks.

For this new life –
stomach rumbling
feelings fluttering
senses wondering
soul awakening –
for this new life
We give You thanks.

Thanksgiving (2) (*mother, family or one voice*)

God of new light
God of new life
You give brightness
in Your likeness;
we praise Your name this day.

Bless this new life
with Your bright light,
together as one
till life is done;
we praise Your name this day.

Healing for the Mother (*family or one voice*)

Peace and healing
love revealing
momentous feeling
joy of birth today.

God, give Your rest
Your strength
Your ease
in the joy of birth today.

God, bring Your touch
Your care
Your health
in the joy of birth today.

God, bless this woman
mother, friend –
peace and healing
love revealing
in the joy of birth today.

The Future (1)

Guardian of life –
preserve new life
infuse with strength
surround with love
protect from harm
open doors of grace
for this little one.
Hold hands, we pray
and walk together day by day
in the avenues of life.

The Future (2)

Looking, yearning, searching
hoping, asking, reaching
the path to You, O Creating One.
Trusting your way
trusting the day
You give to us, O Gracious One.
Bless this child
guard the future
shape the spirit
to love You truly, O Faithful One,
who brings the miracle of life.

Transition

A new presence in the world
    another being, another laugh, another cry.
A new presence coming home
    bringing need, bringing joy, bringing change.
A new presence in our hearts
    developing, connecting, growing.
A new presence for the world
    making space for the spark of God.
A new blessing for the world
    another way to know our God.

Good Health (*unison*)

Child of God, may you know good health
in spirit, mind and body.
Child of God, may you know great love
in spirit, mind and body.
Child of God, may you know sound wisdom
in spirit, mind and body.
Child of God, may you know your Creator
in spirit, mind and body.
For ever.

Sleep *(parent(s) or guardian(s))*

Sleep, little tiny child
sleep as the wind blows
sleep as the seedling grows
sleep, little tiny child.
Sleep in the Creator's care
sleep with dreams so fair
sleep, little tiny child.
Sleep in the cradle place
sleep in the safest space
sleep, little tiny child.
Sleep in this place of peace.

Family Blessing (1) (*one voice*)

Blessed is new life in this family,
blessed is new presence in community.
Blessed is the small one who graces us with joy,
blessed is newborn love for us all.

Family Blessing (2) (*unison or one voice*)

We pray for blessing on each one here
for sister, brother, parent, child
for hands and holding
for love connecting
we pray for blessing on each one here.

Grandparents' Blessing
(*for grandparents in family gathering or alone with child*)

We give thanks for the family growing,
  we bless our God for wisely knowing
the place and time this child may be
  the miracle of life for us to see
our generations move on and on
  with our Sustainer, our Holy One.
Bless this child with Spirit of love eternal,
  bless this child with peace of life eternal.

Ritual for Naming
(*The leader may wish to discover the significance of the name before the ritual.*)

Leader   What name shall this child have?
Parent(s) The name shall be *name*.

Leader   In the presence of the Almighty One, we name
this child *name*. Parent(s), may your richest
blessing surround this child – in thought, word
and deed. May God's glorious intentions guide
this child to fulfil the call of this name day by
day and year by year.
**Parent(s) May *name* know all nourishment, all wisdom,
all guidance that we (I) can give with the help
of God's strength and grace.**

Leader   In the name of the One who names us all
as unique and precious children,
may the blessing of Creator, Christ and Holy Spirit
be upon you and your child
from this moment onward. **Amen.**

Dedication (*for use in the home, possibly in conjunction with the naming ritual; subject may be made plural as appropriate*)

Leader	Who brings this child before God?
Parent(s)/ Guardian(s)	**We (I) do.**

Leader	In the name of the One who is most holy, we have come together to dedicate this child to the Creator's care and blessing. May the holiness of the Almighty rest in this place, on this new creation, bringing love and peace knowing no bounds.
All	**We dedicate *name* to you, Sustaining and Redeeming Presence. May this child's life be dedicated to your guidance. May this child serve you in meaningful ways, as the great servants in times of old who heeded your call. In the name of the One whose voice calls all people.**
Leader	This child is a child of God, presented in the name of the Holy Spirit, dedicated to the Giver of Life. **Amen. So be it.**

EARLY YEARS

Scripture: Deuteronomy 6.4–8; Matthew 18.1–5;
Mark 10.13–16; Luke 2.22–40

Good Health

God, bring good health
  to the young one I know.
God, bring good health
  to the young one I love.
God, bring good health
  to the young one I cherish.
God, bring good health
  to the young one I entrust
  to You.

Safety

Rough and tumble, playing hard
breathing, laughing, learning.
Growing fast, seasons pass
praying, hoping, feeling.

Keeping safe, having fun
learning limits, knowing 'no' –
living 'yes', eluding harm
breathing, laughing, learning.

TEENAGE YEARS

Scripture: Jeremiah 1.4–8; Luke 2.40–51

Good Health

O Great Caregiver,
bring good health to the growing,
good sense to the striving,
good soul to the searching.
O Great Caregiver,
bring clarity to the mind,
charity to the heart,
strength to the body,
so we may serve You well.

Safety

Before the day's break
    may my child know safety.
Before the day's middle time
    may my child know safety.
Before the day's closing
    may my child know safety.
Before the nighttime
    may my child know safety.
During the deep sleep
    may my child know safety.
In all the living times
    may my child know safety.

Studies (*a prayer to be said by or with a young person*)

Knowing One,
help me focus on knowing
yet bring me wisdom beyond knowing.
Centre me on the task at hand,
find me illumined by all tasks before me
in Your wisdom and your persistence;
be in me, Knowing One.

Discernment (*a prayer to be said by or with a young person*)

In the choices,
   in the challenges,
on the roads I walk,
keep me with You
   Guiding God
so I may hear Your voice.
In the choices,
   in the challenges,
on the paths I tread,
help me know You
   Gentle God
so I may do Your will.

Family and Friends
(a prayer to be said by or with a young person)

For those who are dear to me
I give thanks.
For those who support me
I give thanks.
For those who challenge me
I give thanks.
For those who love me
I give thanks.
For those I love
I give thanks.

Teach me thanksgiving in all that I do,
teach me thanksgiving for all gifts from You.

GRADUATION

Scripture: 1 Samuel 3.15-20; Isaiah 48.6-7; 1 Corinthians 1.4-9

Thanksgiving

We dedicate work and study time
  to you, O God.
Endurance, challenge and gifts come
  from you, O God.
The time has come to move ahead
  with you, O God.

Bless all that is behind
bless all that is ahead
bless all that is, today.
With thanks in our hearts
and praise on our lips
we thank You, O God, for the joy
  of this glorious day.

The Future

For all that shall become
for all that may be
for all that shall be known
for all reality
for all there is to hear
for all there is to see
   for promise
   for hope
   for love
   for peace
we give our thanks to Thee.

Transition (*for a young person*)

Everlasting One, call forth the adult in me
   to preserve the child, yet know responsibility.
Ever-present One, call forth the courage in me
   to face the future, and find possibility.
Ever-knowing One, call forth the faith in me
   to trust, to know, that You provide for me.
Ever-loving One, call forth the hope in me
   to know Your call, and serve You faithfully.

LEAVING HOME

Scripture: Ruth 1.15-19a; 1 Kings 19.19-21;
Matthew 28.17-20; Mark 1.16-20

The Future

One door closes, another opens –
the time of change is upon us.
One door opens, another closes –
the future lies ahead of us.
One room for leaving, another for arriving –
possibility a promise.

Keeper of the House, bless the passageways
the openings and closings
and lead us where we need to be.

Transition

Mysterious One,
there is no growth without change;
with change, there is promise of growth.
May joy and sadness, intermingled,
be the whisper of Your presence
in this time of change.

WEDDING

(for planning time, public announcement or family gathering prior to the wedding)
Scripture: Song of Solomon 2.10–14, 16a; John 2.1–11;
Colossians 3.13–17

Joining Together

We praise God who connects all that is living,
we praise God who rejoices in those who marry,
we praise God who blesses all who find love.
Rejoice and be glad, for God is leading
rejoice and be glad, for God is blessing
 those who have found each other
 those who will join together
all that they are –
 all that they will be.
We praise God!

The Future

As the old passes away
and the future opens its gates
may this marriage become a place of
   depth, grace and care
one for the other.
As the old passes away
and life finds new meaning
may this marriage show others
   faith, hope and love
two for all others.

Difficulty

In the difficult times,
have mercy, Understanding One.
Grant Your wisdom
   Your patience
      Your honesty
         Your clarity
to those who face each other.
May they know You in their pain,
may they know You in their anger.
Have mercy, Understanding One,
on those who face each other.

RETIREMENT

Scripture: Deuteronomy 4.9; Matthew 6.34; Matthew 7.7–9

The Past

All that has unfolded from then till now
all that has developed from then till now
all that has come to pass from then till now
   has done so in Your sight, God of the Ages.
For events of great joy
for events of great sorrow
for events changing life completely,
   we give You thanks, God of Purpose.
We have learned
we have loved
we have yearned
we have moved
   through it all, God of Definition.
So now we look forward, living fully
   asking Your blessing for opportunity ahead,
   God of Hope and new beginnings.

Transition

You brought us through life's passages, Journeying One,
  and You bring us through this door.
You brought us through transitions, Guiding One,
  and You bring us to new horizons.

Uncertainty collides with purpose,
leisure measures busyness.
Bring Your meaning to this new place,
  as we walk toward a new land,
  following Your lead.

The Future

The gift of life is full of hope,
the gift of life is full of depth;
the experience of life brings forth wisdom,
the experience of life brings forth patience;

Grant that these qualities of life grow ever more meaningful
  in the days to come,
so each day is joyful, each day is full,
  each day brings forth the spark of You.

Sense of Purpose

Divine One,
All that Was, and Is, and Will soon Be,
what purpose do You have for me?
I am older than I used to be –
what surprise bring You now to me?

God of Ages, what do You see?
What can I do for You, for me?
How might I follow paths You see?
Grant Your grace, Your blessing on me.

LOSS

Scripture: Psalm 130; Isaiah 40.1–8; John 14.1–4, 18–20;
1 Corinthians 15.51–7

Parent (*to be read quietly and slowly*)

> For the one who influenced me so greatly
> for the one who told me things I never knew
> for the one who made an impact on my striving
>   I give thanks.
>
> In this time of loss and mourning
> in this time of dread and sadness
> in this time of change and challenge
>   be with me.
>
> I reach to You for my loved one
> I reach to You for life beyond
> I reach to You for comfort near –
>   hear my prayer
>   hear my prayer
>   hear my prayer.

Partner

Why, O God, is my friend gone?
What, O God, is this thing called death?
Where, O God, has my loved one gone?
How, O God, do I live with death?

Bless the one who walked with me
through life's trials, joys and surprises.
Bless the one who talked with me
through life's travails, hopes and sunrises.
Bless the one who listened with me
through life's denials, dreams and decisions.
Bless the one who has gone from me
though now living again and whole.
Bless the life that opens here for me:
may I know its hope and beauty
    as You walk, talk and listen with me –
while You are with my loved one too.

Sibling (*brother/sister or a name may be substituted for 'sibling'*)

Bless the soul of my sibling
who knew me as a child.
Bless the one who I called *name*
who knew me as a child.

God's light be with my sibling
and in the space left behind.
God's care be with my sibling
and with those who grieve.

May s/he find the peace of God
and know no sorrow ever.
May s/he find the love of God
as we bless *name* for ever.

Friend

In all life, there lives vision.
May we know the vision of Your life
in the time of death,
for one who served
for one who walked
    beside us.
Peace to our friend.
Peace to our living.
Peace for the future.
Peace from the past.
Peace today
    in the name of Your Love.

Part Two

ADDITIONAL SPECIAL OCCASIONS

INTRODUCTION

Oftentimes, people mark special occasions with a party or a meal. For any who are open to God's joy or God's guidance in such celebratory or transition times, prayers call forth a sense of centredness. This section includes celebration prayers, which may be accompanied by a reading of Psalms (scriptural prayers) or other Scriptures. Each prayer is to be personalized with names specific to the occasion. May God's hand be in all of life's events.

Scripture: Psalm 33; 34; 65-7; 81; 92; 96-7; 103; 111; 117; 138; 146-8; 150

ADOPTION

God bless the child who comes to us
God bless the trust of life to us
God bless the love of life to us
God bless the child who comes to us.

God grant that we may care enough
God grant that we may love enough
God grant that we may share enough
God bless the child who comes to us.

God give this child all You will
God love this child all You will
God bless this child all You will
God bless the child who comes to us.

ATTENDING UNIVERSITY/COLLEGE

For the knowledge one can gain
for the gift of work well done
for transition You sustain
we give thanks, O Wisest One.

For the safety and the courage
for the learning and the fun
for the study undiscouraged
we give thanks, O Wisest One.

Mark each day with strength and hope
mark each day with knowledge won
mark each day with broadened scope –
we give thanks, O Wisest One.

BAPTISM

(To be used when planning a baptism, or in a service itself. 'Her' or 'his' may be substituted for 'the'.)

Holy Spirit of God, come to this child –
open the soul to Your guiding.
Holy Spirit of God, prepare this child –
open the soul to Your blessing.
Holy Spirit of God, surround this child –
open the soul to Your loving.
Holy Spirit of God, protect this child –
open the soul to Your cleansing.
Holy Spirit of God, nurture this child
with Your eternal presence.

CHANGE OF PROFESSION

For a leap into change,
for the newness of work,
for a focus on You,
   we pray, O God.
For shift in definition,
for defining of profession,
for profession of the faith,
   we pray, O God.
For the wonder of newness,
for the newness of work,
for the work of Your realm,
   we pray, O God.

COMMITMENT

Giver of Life,
let me give my soul –
all that keeps me whole – to You.
Let me give my heart –
all that I impart – to You.
Let me give each dream –
all that I esteem – to You.
Give to me Your ways
all my waking days
    and we will share a promise – me and You.

CONFIRMATION
(*may be read in the singular or plural*)

One drop of water to cleanse,
another to fill the soul.
Another brings forth a sense
of becoming wholly whole.

Bless this time of confirmation,
God who saves us all –
'tis the time of affirmation
for our greatest call.

'Remember your baptism', comes the word
'be made whole and holy' –
these words I have finally heard
and I affirm them truly.

FEAST

We give our Provider thanks and praise
for all that is before us.
We give our heartfelt gratitude
for all that is behind us.
We give our joy, our pain, our love
and all that is within us
to the One who brings such gifts
to all who are before us.
Thanks be to God for this great day
and let all the people say –
AMEN!

FOSTER-PARENTING

A new child has come to us
seeking care and love.
A new child has come to us
seeking a place to be.
A new child has come to us
seeking shelter, seeking nurture.
A new child has come to us
seeking purpose, seeking safety.
May God provide what this child seeks
through me, through us together.

NEW HOME

May the blessing of this home
and all the space within
bring such great shalom
that the Spirit will come in.
May the blessing of this home
always keep the hearth aflame;
that all of those who wander
may find welcome and remain.

NEW JOB

God, grant wisdom and courage for a new day,
God, grant wisdom and courage for the new work;
God, grant care and attention to tasks before me,
God, grant care and attention to colleagues and friends;
God, grant vision and energy for the present,
God, grant vision and energy for the future;
God, grant me Your peace amidst it all.

PRIZE-GIVING AND AWARDS

All are gifted in Your sight, Creator.
All are worthy in Your name.
In this place, we honour Your creation;
in this space, we lift up Your blessings.
For those named today
   in their talent and their diligence
we give You thanks.
For those to be named in the future
   in their promise and their hope
we give You thanks.
For those who have gifts and talents beyond the scope
   of what we honour here
we give You thanks.
For each one present and each one absent
we give You thanks.

PROMOTION

May the time and energy spent at work
  be blessed to You, O God.
May the hopes and dreams that bring promising future
  be blessed to You, O God.
May the change of place, perspective and focus
  be blessed to You, O God.
May Your blessing be upon me
  in new responsibility
  today and tomorrow, O God.

RELOCATION
(*one voice or unison*)

Everlasting One,
as roots are pulled from the ground,
as the seasons turn,
so too does human life change.
Grant peace and courage
to all who know change,
that opportunity bear new fruits
and new place foster new roots
so life may become centred once again.

Everlasting One,
send down new roots,
hold still as the seasons turn,
be present for all in this time of change.
Grant love and excitement
to each one here
that new fruits and new roots
strengthen the adventure of life
for ever.

REUNION

Blessed are those who travel far
  to find each other
  to hear the stories
  to renew the friendships kept protected through the years.
Blessed are those who travel near
  to see the changes
  to sing the songs
  to affirm the love that holds on through the years.
Blessed are those who open their doors
  to prepare the way
  to invite the travellers
  to welcome all who come this way, now and through the
    years.
Bless this gathering
  bless this reunion
  bless each one
  through the years
  through the years.

Part Three

ADVERSITY

INTRODUCTION

Those who pray tend to turn to God more frequently when life's adversity comes upon them. Often, these difficult times remind us of older sufferings, so the impact of a current event may be magnified. The tone of these prayers is primarily a search for comfort and guidance. Some prayers address the workings of the human mind, while all directly focus on the human spirit.

Included in this section are two short services to be used in the home or with small groups. The Vigil for the Dying includes an affirmation of baptism and a short communion liturgy to be shared as appropriate. The Service for Healing may also be used in the home or with a small group in a room set aside for worship. Candles and fresh flowers enhance the worship, serving as living symbols of hope. These services have proven useful in ministry for a number of people suffering from AIDS or cancer.

Each prayer may be personalized for a given situation. During the reading, periods of silence are meant to be incorporated. Silence can release the feelings accompanying any adversity. May all these prayers and services give hope through difficult times.

Scripture: Psalm 23; Psalm 130; Matthew 11.28-30

ABANDONMENT

Life-companion,
to one abandoned
left behind or pushed away,
bring Your sense of safety
bring Your sense of comfort
to a heart crying in the wilderness.

In the midst of loneliness
in the darkness and by day,
bring Your sense of nurture
bring Your great empowerment
to a soul crying in the wilderness.

May our hands reach out
may our lives touch this one
bringing safety, comfort
bringing nurture, power
in Your name –
to a soul crying for Presence.

ABUSE

(may be used as responsive reading in a group or with an individual, or read in one voice)

Scripture: Isaiah 59.6b-8, 15b-17; Lamentations 3.1-24; Micah 6.8

For the one who is hurting,
we cry to You, O Healing One.
For the one who is wondering,
we cry to You, O Revealing One.
For the one who is not safe,
we cry to You, O Protecting One.
For the one who faces the unknown,
we cry to You, O Discerning One.
For the one who can be healed
we cry to You, O Suffering One.

Grant this one light for body and mind.
Grant this one a friend in You.
Grant this one strength of support.
Grant this one courage for change.
Grant this one relief from isolation.
Grant this one freedom from bondage.
Grant this one healing of heart and soul.

In Your wisdom, we cry to You, O Comforter of the Suffering.

ACCIDENT

We pray for our loved one,
we pray for the stranger too –
we pray for those wondering
   what shall come to pass.
We pray for the injured,
we pray for the rescue –
we pray for Your workings
   in what shall come to pass.
We pray for the hurting,
we pray for the waiting –
we pray for the healing
   in hope that all shall be well.

ADDICTION

An unholy grip has come upon one
beyond all sense and control;
God bring Your strength to this one
and sanctuary to let go.
An unholy grip has come upon those
who seek to support and care;
God, bring Your wisdom to these ones
and courage to let go.

In the darkest night of despair
may Your help come upon one
who is captured, held hostage
in an unholy realm;
God bless this one with freedom.
God bless this one with recovery.
God bless this one with care,
God bless each one with care.

AIDS (1)

We call on strength
   for one who lives day to day,
we call on strength
   for one who suffers day to day,
we call on comfort
   for one who fights illness,
we call on comfort
   for one who fights despair,
we call on courage
   for the future,
we call on courage
   for the loved ones,
we call on love
   for one who learns
   to hope beyond all hope
   for wholeness.

AIDS (2)
(may be read with a silence after even-numbered lines)

For those living with HIV or AIDS
we lift our prayers to You.
For those living with isolation
we lift our prayers to You.
For those living with prejudice
we lift our prayers to You.
For those living with fear
we lift our prayers to You.
For those living with judgement
we lift our prayers to You.
For those living with brokenness
we lift our prayers to You.
God, in Your mercy,
hear our prayers.

ATTEMPTED SUICIDE

One has walked through the valley of the shadow
    and knows the shadows well.
One has travelled the valley of the shadow
    and knows the shadows well.
One has met despair face to face
    and knows that face so well.
One has entered the darkest time
    and knows that place so well.
Urgently, urgently, we pray to You
    for one not feeling heard
    for one we need to heed.
Urgently, urgently, we pray to You
    to show love and care and comfort
    throughout this journey's length.
Instil Your breath of life into
    the one who calls Your name;
in the times of silence
    dispel all sense of shame.
Your love is needed here
    a voice, a word of truth;
bring these, we pray, O God
    and to this soul, Your care.

ATTENTION DEFICIT

For minds that move so fast
impressions that whirl on past
for mood-swings high and low
bodies ever on the go
    we ask for focus and for peace.
For tempers running high
for tiredness often nigh
for behaviour isolation
for friends' desperation
    we ask for breakthrough and for care.

In Your mercy, bring attention
to this one who needs You now;
may we know how to act
to help this one find peace.

CANCER

As the body fights for life
as the mind fights for life
as the soul fights for life
may Your healing touch be here.

As the days remain uncertain
as the nights lie dark and long
as dear ones become more precious
may Your healing touch be here.

In the days of shadows
in the nights
in all time
may Your healing touch bless this one,
may Your boundless love know this one,
may Your steadfast peace grace this one,
in all ways, in all ways.

CAREGIVING

In the name of the Healer,
bring strength to the carer,
in the name of the Healer
bring relief to the giver,
in the name of the Healer
bring courage to the carer,
in the name of the Healer
bring rest to the giver,
for You are the Giver of Care –
    and in adversity, You are with us.

COMA

In the silence
in the darkness
lies one not truly here.
'Midst the waiting
'midst the hoping
lies one not truly here.
With each breath
with each prayer
we lift up the one before us.
For God, You are here
in ways we do not know how to be:
in the silence
in the darkness
we pray that You are truly present.

DANGER

Great Protector,
Your Spirit to one in need.
Great Protector,
Your Safety to one in need.
Great Protector,
share paths avoiding harm.
Great Protector,
spare ones nearing harm.
Great Protector,
hear this cry;
Great Protector,
be close by.

DEATH OF A CHILD
(all prayers may be personalized with names)

Scripture: Jeremiah 31.15; 2 Corinthians 1.3-4

Abuse

In the name of God
  forgive us all
in the name of God
  forgive us all
for the harm that leads to death.

In the name of God
  hear our cry
in the name of God
  hear our cry
for strength, for change, for life.

In the name of God
  break the cycle
in the name of God
  break the cycle
of abuse and misused power.

In the name of God
  care for this child
in the name of God
  heal this child now;
heal us all, we pray.

Accident

We stand before You asking –
O God, where is Your justice?
How could this be?
Our young one has been taken from us.
Out of the depths we cry to You,
we wait for You, our souls wait for You.
We lift our cries to You.

As Christ welcomed the little children
we pray that our child be welcomed in You;
bring Your consolation
assure Your resurrection
and grant us Your peace.

Alcohol/Drug Overdose

We lift our eyes to You, Unknown One
hoping to find reason.
We lift our eyes to You, Great One
daring to ask for solace.
We lift our eyes to You, Deep One
seeking to find answers.
We lift our eyes to You, Suffering One
asking to find purpose.
Bless our lost one, we pray now;
bless our lost one, in Your name.

Rid us of those things which kill
rid us of those things which kill
ease our guilt, our anger
ease our grief, our confusion
bring comfort amidst the questions.

Cot Death

Quietly, our little one slipped away
to rest with You, O God.
We struggle to believe;
we call to You, O God.
Break through the denying,
break through the grieving
with Your hand of comfort, O God.
There was much for which to hope,
there was much love all around;
these are gone with our little one.
We pray that we can help each other,
we pray that anger and despair
will find their place;
we give You these feelings too.
Help us take Your hand
and the hands of others
so light breaks through despair.
Bless us now,
bless our little one,
help us make our homes in You.

Eating Disorder

For the inner tyranny
based on outer expectation
of 'acceptable' body, mind and soul,
we repent, O God.

For the one who was not free
from messages all round, speaking
of 'acceptable' body, mind and soul,
we pray, O God.

For the one who heard inner words
that cried 'unacceptable'
we ask Your unconditional love, O God.

For those of us left behind,
we pray in our emptiness
we pray in our grief
we pray we might address this injustice
that takes young and old needlessly.
We ask for Your forgiveness, Your comfort.
We ask that we may know Your grace and love.

Illness

May Your healing touch be with one
   who suffered.
May Your new life be with one
   who died.
For Christ knew the meaning of suffering,
and Christ died, and came to live again.

May Your healing touch be with us
   who suffer.
May Your new life be with us
   who grieve.
For Christ knew the meaning of suffering,
and Christ can bring us hope again.

Miscarriage

Mysterious One,
the child forming
has been taken away.
The child in womb
has gone to You.
The emptiness is great,
filling body and soul
with numbness, then pain.
Be with this mother,
hold her near,
for a relationship has broken
and the body has betrayed.
In time, bring wholeness
through the grief.
In time, bring hope
through the darkness.
And bless her body, mind and soul.
Bless her child, now made whole.

Stillbirth

Expecting life,
we now know death;
may we know more than death, O God.
Expecting joy,
we now know pain;
may we know more than pain, O God.
Expecting love,
we now know emptiness;
may we know more than emptiness, O God.
Expecting hope,
we now know despair;
may we know more than despair, O God.
Receive this child in Your care,
bless this child whom we barely knew,
renew our faith
renew our hope:
    be with us in our grief, O God.

Suicide

Lives are woven so intricately together
and death comes unexpectedly, tearing the weave.
In the time of tearing
we pray for Your gift of grace, Your gift of peace.

For our loved one who travelled in the depths –
   new hope
for our loved one who could not see light –
   bright light
for our loved one who felt alone –
   pure love
for our loved one who preferred to die –
   pure grace.

In the time of tearing
we call for Your forgiveness, for Your care,
for we did not hear until too late,
for we did not see the valley where our loved one travelled.
In the time of grief,
in the time of confusion,
in the time of guilt,
grant Your mercy, Your steadfast mercy, we pray.

Violence (*may have a time of silence before the last line*)

Tender One,
care for our child,
hold our child in Your arms
for it is a safe place.
Gentle One,
forgive the violence,
steer us clear of hate
for hate claims lives.
Compassionate One,
forgive the ugliness,
help us stand for peace
to make this place safe.
Loving One,
know us as we grieve,
for there are no words
to make it better –

End the violence.

War

Children of war
children of war
may you find peace now
   peace beyond this life
   peace beyond fighting
   peace beyond boundaries
   peace beyond pain.
Children of war
children of war
our prayer for you
   is peace
   is life
   is love
   is hope.
Our prayer for all is peace.

DEATH

Abuse

The fear and pain are over now
for Your servant;
the tragedy of victim's plight
still haunts us all.
Suffering God, You are present now
for Your servant;
be present to us here
in our anger
in our pain
in our helplessness
over the loss of a loved one.
When we did not hear the cries, forgive us.
When we did not see the signs, forgive us.
When we looked the other way, forgive us.
When we tried to help, and could not, we needed You.
When abuse took control, we could not find You.
We pray for Your servant who rests now in safety.
We pray for future justice,
that You bring courage to fight abuse.

Accident

Approaching You
  we cry out our 'why'
approaching You
  we don't know what to say
approaching You
  we know only what we feel
approaching You
  with tears
  with anger
  with a sense of injustice
approaching You
  for help
  for sense
  for meaning
  for comfort amidst tragedy
approaching You
  seeking answers
  seeking a companion for the road of grief.

Alcohol/Drug Overdose

The body is broken
the breath is gone.
The substance has destroyed
the one looking
to alter state of mind.
Forgive this tragedy
forgive our ignorance.
Know our helplessness
know our despair.
Keep our loved one
keep this one safe
in Your arms
in Your heaven.
Heal the broken place
heal the brokenness
on Your earth
amidst this time of tragedy.

Drowning

The danger is past
the struggle is finished
we pray for strength to cope.
May breath of life
may beat of heart
be known again in God's arms.
We pray for our loved one
we share our loss
we make this day a memory.
Fill us with Your breath, O God
fill us with Your hope, O God
fill us with Your promise, O God
that You remain with us,
even as our loved one has gone.

Eating Disorder

May our loved one find a way home now
the anguish of compulsion is over.
We commit this one to You
in body, mind and spirit
so that wholeness springs forth
and resurrection fullness reigns.
We commit our lives to You
and ask for release from
guilt and shame;
bring us comfort in the empty times
fill us with Your Spirit.

Illness

For the one who has passed on,
weakness is now strength
fear is now courage
affliction is now wholeness
despair is now hope
loneliness is now companionship.
For the resurrection of life, we give thanks.
For our weakness, strength
for our fear, courage
for our affliction, wholeness
for our despair, hope
for our loneliness, You.
For the comfort You bring, we give thanks.

Old Age (1)

Life has been full
with heights and depths and plateaux
life has been full
with adventures and stories and people
life has been full
with sickness and health and care
life has been full
has been lived well
and now new life has begun.

Old Age (2)

Welcome Your servant home, O God
with promise of life eternal.
Welcome Your servant home, O God
with joyful hospitality.
Remember Your loved ones here, O God
with tender, constant care.
Remember Your loved ones here, O God
with peace past understanding.
Fill us with Your presence, O God
bring us to Your love
fill us with Your healing, O God
bring us to new faith.

Suicide

Where there is hopelessness, there is tragedy.
God of all time, love these who gather to grieve.
God of all peoples, let your comfort flow through
those who have unanswered questions.
God of the ages, transform this pain into
a growing place,
bring Your hope even in time of tragedy;
where there is hope, there is resurrection.

Violence

Peace be with us all.
Find Your way into the tangled web of our emotions,
    we pray, O God.
Find Your way into our anger
find Your way into our pain
find Your way into our resistance
find Your way into our denial
find Your way into the tangled web of our emotions,
    we pray, O God.
Reassure us that our loved one is at peace
reassure us that our loved one is now whole
reassure us that our loved one is with You
find Your way into the tangled web of our emotions,
    we pray, O God.
Restrain those who do senseless violence
restrain those who foster malevolent anger
restrain those who fight for personal advantage
transform their hearts, transform our hearts;
find Your way into the tangled web of our emotions,
    we pray, O God.
Let us know Your love.

DEPRESSION

Light of the world, it is hard to connect with You
when little has meaning for this one.
Send Your light through the darkness
send Your light to shine in despair
give energy to clear the inner angers.

Light of the world, help us connect with You
to find meaning for this one.
Send Your light to bring meaning
send Your light to bring focus
outside the walls of depression.

Stir life in Your loved one
stir inner purpose too
stir humour and lightness
break through the walls of depression
break through the walls.

DISASTER

O God, You are our help and our hope.
In times of disaster, keep each one safe
in times of recovery, keep each one encouraged.
O God, You are our help and our hope.
We pray for families to stay together
we pray for animals' lives
we pray for plants and earth.
O God, You are our help and our hope.
May destruction become reconstruction
may community draw together
may friendship spring from common adversity
may Your help heal wounds of disaster.
O God, You are our help and our hope
in years past, and ages yet to be.

DISILLUSIONMENT

When dreams begin to die
  and visions wane
keep us from becoming cynical
  in our disappointment;
keep us from becoming lifeless
  in our disillusionment.
Show us dreams of new life
  and visions transformed
so that we are filled with hope
  and joy and laughter
  with our trust in You.

DIVORCE

God of infinite love,
pour out Your understanding here.
For new beginnings
for healing of hurts
for holding happy memories
for letting go of sad memories
for releasing feelings of despair
for nurturing confidence
for forgiveness of wrongdoing
for growth in new life
for all who love this one
for friends and family
for acceptance of the new
for all these things we pray
in the name of the Light.

DYING (1)

Facing the unknown
    we pray for safe journey
    from this world to the next
facing the unknown
    we pray for painless passage
    from this world to the next.

Be with our loved ones
    keep them safe and well
forgive us our sins
forgive us our wrongs
    and receive us into Your grace.
May we be assured that Your promise is true
    that You wait for each of us.

Facing the unknown
    we pray for safe journey
    from this world to the next
facing the unknown
    we pray for painless passage
    from this world to the next.

DYING *(2)*

Bless the breathing of this one
who has given much to life.
Bless the thinking of this one
who has taken much from life.
Bless the feeling of this one
who knows fullness of all life.

In the time of passage
we pray for safe return
to the place of our beginning
the place for which we yearn.
May Your servant know
that You hold safely on;
this journey gathers light
once it has begun.

Your servant travels soon
with Your promises in mind;
we wish our loved one joy
and peace for us behind.

VIGIL FOR THE DYING

(*Communion may be shared, Scripture read, and personal prayers from friends and relatives may be heard. If the person dies at this time, appropriate prayers may be used from this or other resources.*)

Scripture: Psalm 23; 90.1–6; 103; 121; 130; 139.1–18; 146; Isaiah 40.28–31; Luke 24.13–35; John 14.1–4, 18–19, 25–7; Revelation 7.16–17

Prayer

Mysterious One,
we are here to bless Your servant
to acknowledge this time of trial
to renew our spirits
to seek Your peace.
In the name of the Christ.

Scriptures

Memories shared with those present (including the dying if possible).

Prayer

Eternal God,
You knew us before time
You know us now
You will know us in new life.
Bring Your courage to this place
bring Your strength to this place
for the journey through the door of death
to the light of resurrection life.
Bless Your servant here

who prepares to meet You
and know the full glory of new life.
We claim Your promise;
we pray for safe journey
on the way home to You.

Scriptures

Reaffirming one's baptism (optional)

(*Water may be used in the joining of hands.*)

**Today, we affirm our baptism into God's reign on this
  earth.
We remember our baptism and are thankful.
We acknowledge Your grace
as Your Spirit came to dwell in us
setting us in right spirit to be with You.
All praise to You, Redeeming and Sustaining God.
May we remain faithful disciples with each breath we
  take.
So be it.**

Scriptures

Communion Service

May God be with us all.
We give thanks and praise to the Creator of all things.
You called us into being
You provided us with promise
You sustained us in this life

You lead us to the next.
We praise Your holy name.

You sent Christ to us
to let us know You
to show us what love means
to release us from our sins.
As his own death drew near,
he shared one last supper
with his followers and friends.
On that night, he took bread from table
broke it
and said: 'This is my body, broken for you.
Do this in remembrance of me.'
After the supper, he took the cup of wine
and said: 'This is my blood, shed for you.
Drink from it, all of you.
Do this in remembrance of me.'
This day, we remember Christ's acts for us
and call upon the Holy Spirit to bless us here
and bless these elements.
We offer ourselves to You through our communion together,
in the name of Christ.

The Lord's Prayer

Sharing the elements

Take, eat, this is Christ's body, broken for you.
Take, drink, this is Christ's blood, shed for you.

Prayer

It is with humble thanks that we have shared in Your
meal.
As Christ then departed from this world, to the next,
we give thanks for the gift he brought to us.
Bless Your servant here, that in this journey all will be
well
for this one is in communion with You.

Blessing

Peace to you.
Your spirit is in safe hands.
Be at peace.

EATING DISORDER

God, help Your servant find courage
to let go
    of feeling inadequate
    of fear
    of self-distrust.
God, may our loved one find the truth
to let go
    of mixed messages
    of need to control
    of emptiness.
Forgive all who fed falsehood.
Help us to seek justice here.
God, You are the one who brings confidence
God, You are the one who brings health.
Fill us with Your steadfast care
    and never leave us empty again.

FINANCES

When there is little
God bring bread and water.
When there is little
God bring health and shelter.

When there is little
God provide enough.
When there is little
God provide strength.

When there is little
God show us work.
When there is little
God show us relief.

When there is little
God help us find the way.
When there is little
God help us in Your way.

HOMELESSNESS

For people barely surviving on the streets
we pray for safety and for food.
For people cold and weary
we pray for shelter and for warmth.
For the people influencing politics
we pray for insight and compassion.
For the people controlling money
we pray for generosity and graciousness.

May we as people serving You
know that justice is the only way
to find place for people homeless
to find place for each one.
Human dignity is at stake –
we see it well, O God.
We set our faces to the task
with Your guidance, and Your hope.

ILLNESS

Desiring Death

For the weary
we pray for release
for the hopeless
we pray for release
for the one who is content
we pray for release
for the one who is ready
we pray for release.

We pray for death that is a healing
we pray for resurrection that is wholeness
we pray that we might say farewell with love
   and gratitude.
We pray for death died well,
   from life lived well.
We pray for Your protection on this one last
   journey;
we pray for release.

Healing

God, with Your healing, anoint this one who suffers
God, with Your ease, bless this one who feels pain
God, with Your promise, come upon this one who searches
God, with Your strength, breathe upon this one who labours.

A healing touch
a word of ease
a breath of promise
a gift of strength.
These things we ask of You, Long-suffering One, this day.

Service of Healing

Scripture: Psalm 13; 42; 91; 130; Isaiah 35.1–10; Isaiah
40.28–31; Matthew 8.1–13; Matthew 11.28–30; Mark 5.21–43;
Mark 10.46–52; Luke 5.17–26; Luke 7.11–17; Luke 8.43–8;
Luke 17.11–19; John 11.1–44; Acts 5.12–16

Opening scripture

May grace and peace be yours in abundance in the knowledge
of God and of Christ. (2 Peter 1.2)

Prayer

**Healer of the ages,
we lift our loved one to You
for healing – in body, mind and spirit.
May we open our hearts to possibility**

**may we know Your presence in this place
may we find courage and strength to trust
in Your name.**

Scriptures

Prayer for cleansing

Almighty One,
we approach You in quiet awe
we approach You seeking health
we pray for faith to trust
we pray for forgiveness
we pray for cleansing of thought, word and deed.
Make us ready to receive You
in this holy place.

We give thanks for Your anointing
of the ill and the troubled.
Purify us so that we may receive
this oil of healing.
Pour out Your Holy Spirit upon us
and upon this gift
so that we may be made whole in Your name.

*Anointing with oil (participants may want to touch one hoping
for healing if appropriate)*

Leader   (*making sign of the cross on forehead or hands
or both*):
Child of God, I anoint you with oil, in the name of
the holy and triune God, Creator and Healer of
all things.

Those laying hands on person's head or hand:
> **These hands are laid on you, in the name of the holy and triune God, Creator and Healer of all things.**

Leader   May the power of God heal you
>> in body
>> in mind
>> in spirit
>> in relationship.
>> So be it.

Prayer of Thanksgiving

> We are grateful, all-knowing One
> for Your gifts here today.
> Let us know Your peace now
> and live in gratitude
> for the promise of Your presence.

Scriptures

Blessing

> The God who heals you
> bless and keep you.
> The God who knows you
> grant you deep peace.

IMPAIRMENT

Physical

O Perfect One,
we come before You in imperfection
we come before You in impairment
we come before You in frustration
  that all is not as it could be.

In this body, bring strength anew
in this body, bring life anew
in this body, bring Your purpose.
We come before You in hope
  that all can reach its best potential.

Renew mind and spirit
for the daily work
that requires much.
Renew the wonder
of blessings given
in unique ways
  to each one.

Mental

God, You speak to each one
   uniquely.
God, You reach out to each one
   freely.
God, You bless each one
   greatly.
Bless Your servant here today.

For a mind that sees much,
for a mind that knows much,
for a mind that experiences much,
for a mind that can teach much,
we praise Your name.
Teach us, Learned One,
   what You would have us know
   about each other
   and about You.

Spiritual

In the silence of the spirit
we search for You.
In the absence of the presence
we hunger for You.
In the disbelief that You care
we call out to You.

For all that blocks our way to You
we pray for freedom from constraint.
For all that threatens our soul-health
we pray for courage and for strength.
For all that draws us away again
we pray for focus and for power
  to journey toward You.

INFIDELITY

When love has not been lived
and difficulty arises,
when care shifts away from one
and another is found,
God, be present to each one,
God, be present to each one.
When there is betrayal
in more than one direction,
when there is loss of trust
and secrets start to rule,
God, be present to each one,
God, be present to each one.

Give each one a sense of care
to turn and face this sin.
Keep the blame from tearing down
and bring Your wisdom forth.
God, transform each one's heart,
God, transform each one's heart,
    so honesty comes about
    so healing takes its place
    and whatever future brings
    Your name is honoured all ways.

LOSS OF LIMB

A piece of me is missing
a part of me is gone
yet sometimes I feel it
and ever want it back.

In my anger for this loss
in my grief for a limb
I turn my face to You
for strength when I feel weak.

When ready to accept
I call upon Your care
to bring me coping skills
and energy to live well.

PAIN

In the suffering
bring Your strength.
In the suffering
bring Your meaning.
In the suffering
bring release.
In the suffering
bring hope.
God, bless Your suffering servant.

PRISON

O God, be within this place of restraint
where bars and timeclocks rule the day.
O God, be within each person here
who searches for meaning beyond routine.
O God, be within the hearts and minds
of those who simply survive
    so that thoughts of freedom
        from wrongdoing
        from cellblocks
        from temptation
        from blank walls
    become a way of living
    in Your name.

RESTLESSNESS

The winds blow
and do not settle.
The waves crash
and never cease.
The earth rumbles
always wakeful.
The fires burn
consuming much.
The spirit moves
and will not 'light'.
The search is all
search unending
   for illumining
   for discerning
   for direction
   for meaning.
Come, Spirit, come
rest in my own spirit
that my spirit may rest in Yours.

SEPARATION

Partner

For the promise
which comes to end
which cannot mend
we lift our hurt to You.
In new space
in new place
we turn anew to You.
Help find a way
to remake life
to end the strife
and find Your healing ways.
Renew us now
assure us somehow
keep us always with You.

Children

We pray for the children
in time of confusion.
We pray for the children
in time of unknowing.
We pray for the children
when insecurity reigns.
We pray for the children
when they take blame.
We pray for the children
as they question.
We pray for the children
as they strive for love.
We pray for the children
in our thoughtful care.
We pray for the children
in Your tender care.

Custody

When the pulling of a person
begins to be a part of life
God, help the child who is pulled
in the midst of all the strife.

When a child visits one
then returns to other
God, help the child with two homes
to know both father, mother.

As adjustment settles in
and children find their place
may we all be sensitive
to God's redeeming space.

SIN

(The act of repentance may include all four elements below, with silence between each. Prayers may be used in singular or plural form for the penitents, followed by words of reconciliation and thanksgiving by another party; prayers also may be adapted for individual use.)

Penitence

That which I have done
that has harmed others
that has harmed You
that has harmed me
I acknowledge.
I know sorrow.

Confession

These acts and thoughts I confess before God:
(*Silence*)
For all times I have moved against Your will
for all ways I have been destructive
for all people I have manipulated
for all truth I have denied
for all deeds I have done in ignorance
I am sorry.
I pray Your strength to change in these ways,
    so that I can follow Your path more faithfully:
(*Silence*)
God, have mercy, Christ, have mercy, God, have mercy.

Reconciliation

Redeeming One, from whom all blessings flow,
You have promised forgiveness for all who seek it.
Bless this servant with Your steadfast love,
may this servant know Your grace,
and may all be reconciled in covenant relationship
    from this day forward.
Through Your grace, we pray.

Thanksgiving

In the name of the Almighty,
we give thanks!
Our burden is lifted
our lives renewed
our hearts opened
our souls cleansed.
In the name of the Almighty,
we give thanks!

SINGLE PARENTING

In the times of joy for children
  I bring thanksgiving.
In the times of hardship with children
  I bring petition.
In the times when I am alone
  I bring cries for care.
In the times when I am overwhelmed
  I bring desire for rest.
In the times when I am hopeless
  I bring prayers for courage.
In the times I find You here
  I bring thanksgiving.

SUICIDE

No life You made is without meaning
no earthly act is without redeeming.
Through Your grace, take this one home
to a place with no more isolation.

Commit this one to shelter from the storm
and lead this one away from harm.
Sustain us here with Your strength
for our grieving runs deep.

Deliver us from our own guilt
commit us to the love you promise
    in the name of One who suffered
    then brought new life.

UNCERTAINTY

When there is much in front of me
open my eyes that I may see
open my heart that I may discern
what it is You'd have me learn.

When there is much to bring me fear
open my ears that I may hear
open my mind that I may know
where it is You'd have me go.

When there is such deep confusion
open my hands to know communion
open my soul to find the way
keep me near You, come what may.
Keep me near You, day by day.

UNEMPLOYMENT

Despite rejection keenly felt
despite potential not fully realized
despite future bleak and fear-filled
we pray for hope, we pray for work.

In times of hardship, few resources
in times of dreams found limiting
in times of boredom, endless searching
we pray for hope, we pray for work.

We pray that we might know a neighbour
who brings in a ray of light.
We pray that we might find a friend
who walks with us in this place.
We pray that we accept Your help.
We pray for hope, we pray for work.

WAR

God, throughout all time
   human beings have faced each other
   to fight for power and territory.
God, throughout all time
   mothers' children are killed
   fathers' children are killed
   friends are killed
   loved ones are killed.
This time, we have lost one of our own.
We join all the voices who pray for Your comfort,
we join all the voices who pray for Your peace,
we join all the voices who pray for life beyond life
   for our loved one.
We pray that there shall not be war any more.

WEARINESS

When there is no energy left
when all has been seen and done
we know that You call us
to let go.

When rest is greatest peace
when sleep is deepest comfort
we know that You call us
to let go.

You call Your servant to renewal
you call Your servant to find hope.
May we know Your gift of life
brings strength we need.

Teach us to let go.